From the Back Streets to the Front Line

A true story of growing up in Cardiff and travelling through Africa, Italy and Austria in the 2nd World War

by
William Mark Lee

authorHOUSE®

AuthorHouse™ UK Ltd.
500 Avebury Boulevard
Central Milton Keynes, MK9 2BE
www.authorhouse.co.uk
Phone: 08001974150

© 2008 William Mark Lee. All rights reserved.

No part of this book may be reproduced, stored in a retrieval system, or transmitted by any means without the written permission of the author.

First published by AuthorHouse 8/26/2008

ISBN: 978-1-4389-0768-0 (sc)

Printed in the United States of America
Bloomington, Indiana

This book is printed on acid-free paper.

Edited By M.A.Lee

This book is dedicated to my wife Hilda and my Children for their love and support, especially my Son Mark who has made this book possible

CONTENTS

Chapter 1: Childhood Years 1

Chapter 2: Teenage Years 31

Chapter 3: The War Began 35

Chapter 4: Leaving Home 41

Chapter 5: Revenge or Accident 49

Chapter 6: Fear and Training 53

Chapter 7: Abroad for the First Time 59

Chapter 8: The Atlas Mountains 65

Chapter 9: Blida and the Bizerta Excursion 73

Chapter 10: Solerno and the Front Line 79

Chapter 11: The Result of War 87

Chapter 12: The Volturno River 91

Chapter 13: Brush with Death, the First Time 95

Chapter 14: Brush with Death, Second Time 99

Chapter 15: Brush with Death, Third Time and The Tough Guy 103

Chapter 16: Into the Lions Mouth at Solerno 109

Chapter 17: The Front Line Again, or Not 115

Chapter 18: Better Days and XMas Dinner – Hamen Lif.. 121

Chapter 19: Verona – Padua – Genoe – Appiano – Viena and The Russians................ 129

Chapter 20: Klagenfurt and the Germans 141

Chapter 21: Getting Out 145

CHAPTER 1
CHILDHOOD YEARS

I followed our gang across the river, finding a balance between each rounded stone until at once the floor became no more and I was engulfed in dark freezing water. The heat was stripped from my body as I kept going down. At the age of seven I had little idea of the pending death but could hear the echoes of my mother telling me not to go near the river. It got darker and colder as I went deeper and I could do nothing to free myself from descent. In those few seconds I experienced fear for the first time in my life, not anxiety nor worry but raw fear that reaches into your soul and grasps your spirit tight. This was not the last time in my life that I would visit that same purgatory. Time passed and struggling was not in mind until I felt the warmth of someone's grasp on my arms who pulled me up into the light and free from my watery casm, it was my older brother Danny.

About six of our gang, with Danny leading, had been walking across the river Taff to go into the apple orchard of Cardiff Castle. It was a summer evening, about 7 o'clock, the sun was still warm in the evening sky and the air was tainted with summer smoke. I was wearing the dust that can only be attained by a hard day rolling on the ground, climbing anything in site and avoiding the time wasting washing routine mothers like to enforce. As I stepped into the river, following the others, my mind was working on how I would avoid being caught whilst still pinching the most apples. They were crossing the river by walking across a sunken roman wall just under the water, along side which was an old well. I didn't know this and simply followed, as one does.

He pulled me to the bank, as the others looked on. He was much bigger and two and half years older than me. We didn't know about resuscitation methods in those days. When he could see that I would survive he put me on his back and carried me home, which was no mean feat as we lived two miles away. When we arrived home the rewards for his efforts were far from sight, he had a good hiding from my father for not looking after me. "But I saved him from drowning" he kept saying but Dad said "if you had looked after him it would never have happened". I was as surprised as Dan. From that day on, Dan tried not to have me with him.

I was born in 1922 in central Cardiff. Being one of ten children living in a terraced house in Rodney St was fairly normal. The only one younger than myself was my sister Sheila. It was a 3 bedroom house and my parents slept in the big bedroom along with Sheila and Bet who slept together in a single bed. Tom, Dan and myself slept in the other bedroom and Alice and Margaret slept in a single bed in the box room. Mary, my eldest sister slept, or lived, in my Grandmothers house around the corner in Tredegar St.. My other sister Helen, we called her Cissy, went to live with our Aunt Liz in

Swansea, Aunt Liz and her husband Mark had no children. Lastly, John, my eldest brother slept in a single bed at the foot of ours. We did not find this arrangement unusual as others also had to do the same in those days.

George VI Coronation 1937, our street party

There were about twenty terraced houses in the street and about sixty children, mainly teenagers but a good mix all the same. In the summer, the street was packed with children playing different games. In those days before the 1939-45 war the seasons were always well defined. The summer would be sunshine for four months June to September, almost guaranteed, then the autumn, winter and spring always came on time. April we'd have April showers all month and the March winds would blow in March and so on. The changing of the seasons were well defined each carrying an air of excitement, an expectancy of change and a repeat of the good things life brought each time round. We had little money so the things we enjoyed were the important ones, the ones you can't buy.

Summer school holidays were a time of freedom, of exploration, when reputations were made and historical events baked into our lives which would be recounted on street corners and embellished to become larger than life. It was sacrilegious to do any schoolwork or related activity in that period. Those who did were regarded as outsiders and had our collective sympathy. No more than this could be allocated to such a trivial matter, it was regarded as an infringement of our freedom and as such should be scorned an every occasion. In the August school holidays our street gang, fifteen to twenty or more of us, would go to Sophia gardens to swim in the river Taff. In fact that's where I learned to swim, in the shallows at first but before long and still only five or six years of age, I joined the rest. We'd make tents from the old sacking that had been wrapped around sides of bacon. We would collect them from outside the bacon warehouse where they were left thrown on the ground. By the time we got them they would smell pretty strong, but at the time it past unnoticed. They were the nearest we got to a real tent but, tied together with string they did the job. We'd have bread and jam sandwiches, a flagon of water and we'd buy a half penny (about 1/5 of one new pence) worth of sherbet and mix it in the water which gave us our pop for the whole day.

The canal passing through the city centre was also a regular swimming spot. This was a waterway coming to the end of its working life and used in bygone days to move coal, in barges, from mines in the valleys to the docks. The water in the canal was black with coal dust and had dead dogs, rats, cats and other unidentifiable things floating in it. It's inconceivable how we didn't catch a disease but then that's how life goes. From the bridge in Kingsway, a road passing alongside the castle, people would throw half penny's in the canal and Dan and his mates would dive for them to catch them before they reached the bottom. If they reached the muck at the bottom they would be lost.

Barges were towed by a Shire horse on the tow path alongside the canal near the wall of the castle in North Rd, half way down North Rd there was a lock gate and cabin. The operator stayed in the barge whilst being lowered in the lock to the level in the canal so as to carry onto the docks (this area in North Rd is now a car park) taking them past Kingsway Bridge, under the road to the other side and on under Queens St. Overlooking the canal from Queens St was a 6ft high wall with a metal gate in it used for the Shire Horses to go through crossing Queens St to Hills Terrace and Canal St. Horses walked up the ramp to the gate but the canal barge had to be pushed along by the Bargees lying on top of the cabin and walking along the roof of the tunnel until the horse and man and barge met on Hills Terrace canal bank. Horses would then walk towards the Hayes Bridge where there were wide steps from the pavement down to the canal bank. We would visit this area regularly and we all knew children had been drowned in this part of the canal. I remember a priest placing a candle on a piece of wood and waiting until it stopped further down with the flow. A diver would then search and did find a small boy drowned. My brother Tom saved a boy from our street when he fell into the canal. The canal went onto the West Wharf where the banks were wide and many sunny days were spent there swimming.

Marks and Spencer had the front of the shop in Queens St with R S Heaths piano shop on one corner in Charles St, the other corner was held by Wm Fowler auctioneers in Paradise Place. The staff and goods entrance to M&S was half way down Paradise Place just before the old Labour Exchange which M&S took over when the Labour Exchange moved to Westgate St in the late 40's early 50's.

We went to St David's school in David Street (the Worlds Fair building is built on it now). My Mother took me to start in the infants. It was run by Nuns and the Sisters in charge had set up a table in the playground and entered our names and addresses in a ledger. My Mother would be in the entrance to the playground every morning at about 10 o'clock with a jug of tea and some sandwiches for me and for my younger sister, Sheila when she also joined the infants. Few had mothers whose love went so deep, every morning, winter and summer she would be there, it has to be said however, that another three were also regular attendees.

When I moved up to the boy's school, which was in the next building, the classes were huge, as many as 45 or 50 to a class. In the winter we would sit frozen to the bone as there was only one coal fire in the classroom but we daren't complain. The teacher would sit next to it, changing sides to ensure a good all round heat exposure and blocking any heat escape to at least half those in the front row at any one time. Those sitting close to the back were unlucky as they were coldest of all.

Our footwear was laced stud boots. Some didn't have boots so they would be given a pair of boots by the Parish, as it was called (the social security nowadays), but only if the father was dead or unemployed, and there were many unemployed. I've seen some with part of a tyre tread nailed onto the bottom of their boots and others wearing clogs (wooden shoes). Money was very scarce in those days.

In winter I'd rush home from school, only two streets away, and in the passage of our house be blessed with the smell of most beautiful soup in the world. Always delicious, I couldn't have enough of it (I always had a big appetite). My father was a keen practitioner of the art of boxing, many's the man he fought bare fisted and beat in our area (only as a last resort). He made a boxing ring out the back for me, Dan and Tom and also put up a pear shaped punch ball for us to practice on and to develop our arm muscles.

He used the punch ball every day, he could keep a steady rhythm for long periods. He used it to cure his damaged right elbow. He damaged it whilst in France, Dad was in the infantry 'The Welsh Regiment' (same as I was) and he and two mates were buried for two days from a mortar shell, in the Mametz woods, he was in hospital in France for months. He always tried to use that arm to keep it workable. He loved punching the ball, the beat was so regular it sounded like a tap dancer.

I recall being told a story of when he was courting my mother. They were walking towards her house when they could see her father, a quiet man, on the doorstep. A man called O'Leary was upsetting and tormenting him, this man was an Irish bully and braggart of the area. He was sneering and calling my Grandfather names. My father saw this as he approached. He walked up to him slowly and with confidence, he was not afraid, he taught us also never to be afraid, O'Leary stood yelling and screaming obscenities but this had no effect on my father. This was when his boxing practice would pay dividends, he said nothing as there was nothing to be said. They stood face to face, close enough for O'Leary to take the first punch but it was futile as my father saw the intention in his eyes and as his hands moved he blocked and delivered three punches before he could draw another breath.

It was a long cobbled street and he knocked him from one end to the other, with the same rhythm that he had been so used to using every day on the punch bag. When he was satisfied that O'Leary had had enough he was made to apologise to my Grandfather, from that day on he showed respect to the old man.

My Dad was quite inventive so as we didn't have the money he would try to make it. We thought the world of him. The area that we lived in was the same everywhere no one was well off and no one had a wireless, unless it was rented, but on more or less all of streets there was a Pub. Only men allowed in, no women. They could go into the Snug which was a small little room for four people on the side of most Pubs. On most Saturday nights us kids would be in bed waiting for the sound of a fight outside in the street. We would open the windows and have a grand view of the fight, until my Mam would guess we were watching it and then she would be up to shut the window and warn us not to open it again.

My Father would never show himself up. He was a quiet intelligent man, concerned about the boys developments.

From the Back Streets to the Front Line

*Corpis Christi –
Sisters and Brothers Sheila, Danny,
Billy, Tom and Bette*

William Mark Lee

*Corpis Christi –
Sisters and Brothers Alice John,
Mary, Cissie and Margaret*

He also put up a pair of rings for me to pull myself up on and that made me extra strong. My Mother complained when he would make us put the big boxing gloves on and spar up to each other, so he stopped doing that. This was a pity really as he always hoped he would have a son he could train to box. Mam played hell about it she even burned the boxing gloves when Dad had died. Had he lived, me and Dan would have at least been in gymnastics of some sort.

My brother John couldn't get a job so he joined the Welsh Guards stationed in London. He was only 17 years old, Mam was really upset, and he did it without telling anyone. My Dad was unemployed as a Docker unloading cargo. He wasn't employed regularly only when a ship's urgency was paramount. There were hundreds of Dockers just waiting for their turn to work. He came home one evening his clothes and his face covered in red dust. He'd been unloading iron ore his head was bandaged and he told my Mother the hook of the crane had hit him. He'd been taken to the Cardiff Royal infirmary and they just bandaged his head, dressed the cut and sent him home. That bang on the head would grow into a tumour and kill him in later years. He went to work the next day because he would not get any money staying home, even-though the injury was the fault of the dock's crane driver. There was no such thing as sickness benefit then.

Mam was a hard working, loving woman but when you're young it's all taken for granted, only when you get older do you realise the sacrifices she made for us. To survive she even made up our front room into a little shop selling sweets, groceries vegetables and sticks. She'd make toffee apples just to get some money to exist because my Dad's job wasn't constant. Although he'd walk down to the docks every morning at 5:30 a.m. hoping to be employed, only now and again would there be work. Mam was owed so much money by the neighbours that she had to shut up shop.

During the 1914 -1918 Great War Dad was away in France, in the trenches like millions of men, my mother still had to feed and clothe five children. Often, as early as 5 o'clock in the morning, she would go to Edward England's Potato Wharf in the West dock. She would push a sack truck with two one hundred weight sacks of potato from the Tindel St Wharf up the hill in Bute road to the potato warehouse on the Hayes. Lorries could not be used as the there was no petrol due to the war. After working three hours she would return home to get the children fed, dressed and off to school. Life was very hard in those days people didn't have help from the government like today, people could and did starve.

I remember my Dad being carried on a stretcher down the stairs and into an ambulance and taken to Chepstow all military hospital and that the last we children ever saw of him. That would have been 1931 because he died February 16th 1932. The funeral stands out in my mind. In those days the hearse was drawn by four black horses with ostrich feathers placed on top of their head held by a black band around the forehead. Following this was a small enclosed carriage of four people drawn by one horse. Family and neighbours walked behind these all the way through the Hayes to Kingsway right up to Cathays cemetery where he was buried. It was a never ending walk for us youngsters. In those days everyone went in Black. Often they would get in to debt to buy the clothes and men would also take the day off work in respect, not to like nowadays just attending for an hour or so and then rushing back to work. They couldn't afford to lose a day's pay but had to in the old days. Dad was 51 years old when he died Mam couldn't claim anything because of his accident in work which had caused the tumour which killed him. You had to have money for a solicitor and she had none.

On the morning after he died we were dressing, ready to go to school when there was a loud knock on our front door. Mam said that sounds like a policeman knocking, it was and Mam took him into the front room. He said dad had passed away in the night. Mam screamed and collapsed crying to the chair. We were all crying, I'll never forget that morning. The policeman said to Tom your man of the house now.

Although John was older than Tom, John was in London, in the army. John was sent for. In that year there were two more deaths in the family. My

Grandfather Quirk, who lived around the corner (my Mother's Father) and my Uncle Eddy Fitzgerald, who lived across the street from us (my Aunt Jules' husband). So Mam had a terrible year in 1932.

MA

At the start of our summer school holidays, third week in July to mid-September, we all would have a pair of daps, canvas covered rubber sold laced shoes. What a lovely feeling with those daps on, you could run as fast as a deer around the streets or play rounders so much better than in school boots.

I had a bike which I thought was great, I had made it myself. It was a man's bike frame with two small round pram wheels on it and a rolled up piece of sacking for a seat. I would have to run and jump on it as it had no chain. It was the envy of the kids down the street. If you were lucky you owned a hoop, which was a bicycle wheel with no spokes in it, you just ran round, a long side it, hitting it with a stick to keep it rolling. If you were really lucky, you had a car tyre which, instead of the bicycle wheel, this was regarded as best of all.

Another vehicle that I made was a bogey. This was a plank of wood, four pram wheels and axles. The front axle could move either right or left to guide the bogey. A pole was used to push it along and an open box was used as the seat. Kids would queue up to push you.

Christmas was a happy and marvellous time. This did not mean plenty of toys. We had maybe two toys but always, my mother filled our stockings with oranges, apples and nuts. The happy close family feeling was great. Us children would try and save (halfpenny at a time) one shilling by Christmas to buy our sweets with. We'd take a shoe box to Chapples, our sweet shop, and buy half a penny's worth of ten assorted little bags of sweets and take them home and put them on top of Mam's wardrobe until Christmas day. For Christmas dinner my mother, somehow, would always have a goose. That was the top bird in those days as turkeys had yet to come from America. Some families down our street would be lucky to have rabbit and some would have no Christmas dinner at all. We would go to the pantomime maybe once and no one sent Christmas cards to anyone else, it was simply not done. Our family were not rich, but, we always had plenty of food and good clothes.

When I think of it, boys only wore long trousers when they had left school and started work. Boys in school, must have been very cold in winter because we wore short trousers all of the time. The other item all boys wore was a jersey, some wore them until they were full of holes and dropped off. They were not made up of wool but a form of nylon.

Sheila was an excellent swimmer, she was in St Davis School Swimming Champions team. I remember on one occasion when the Cardiff schools (Catholic) held their Gala to see who was the best team of four (I think) Catholic schools. It was held in Guildford Crescent swimming baths, it was the only one we had in those days. It was held on a summers evening and hundreds of schoolchildren were outside the baths waiting to see if their school team won.

An official came out after the races were finished and said St David's have won the Gala. We all cheered and waited for the team to come out with the first prize called 'The Rose Bowl'. They were carried on the shoulders of the boys up to the convent at the top of David St next to St David's church hall (where the Arena is now). Sheila also won a silver medal and two bronze ones. The Sisters came out to welcome the team and say how proud St David's was of them. When the team was carried from the swimming pool we were all singing our school song "Who said St David's couldn't win, St David's couldn't win at all and so on". Sheila will remember that evening I am sure, sad to say that many years later because of pain in her knee medical specialists advised to put her leg in plaster which held it rigid resulting in her joints becoming interlocked and it become impossible for her to bend her knee ever again. All this happened when I was abroad for 3 ½ years. When I came home on leave after 3 years or so and I saw her leg in plaster I played hell, but I'm sure it was too late after years kept straight. Even I, with no medical knowledge could see it was a bad thing to keep it locked for this length of time. As I said, as good a swimmer as she was she never swam as well ever again, due to ignorant doctors.

No one had a toilet inside their house they were all outside. We would walk from the back door down the back garden, about 35 ft, to the toilet. Next door to the toilet would be the wash house, where my mother would boil up all the family clothes every Monday. She would light a fire under a big cast iron drum shaped like an upside down dome. The water would be brought to a boil and the whites and other clothes boiled in turn in this way. Then she had a big wooden roller called a mangle, which was used to press all the water out of the clothes. No one helped her.

In the winter we would wait until we were bursting before we went to the toilet in the dark, we would take a candle but the wind would always manage to blow it out. You would always ask for someone to go with you but no one would ever agree. Although, Mam would sometimes go with you until you got into the toilet then she would go back into the house. You would rush as fast as you could to do your business and run to get back into the house. This often resulted in wet legs. We had no electricity in our houses so a candle was always used especially when going to bed., it was marvellous when we eventually had electricity put in to switch on the electric light.

My mother used to save for months with Lermons Savings for all our Corpus Christi clothes. This was for Tom, Dan, Bet me and Sheila. In those days you had to pay before you received the articles from the shop, so one would have to save every week to buy what you required. Lermons was a big drapery stall on the Hayes Bridge road who stocked Roman Catholic Corpus Christi suits, shoes for the boys and white dresses and veils for the girls. They had a lot of trade from our area. There was no such a thing as have now and pay later like today's shops, which was just as well because they would never have got to pay it. Once people had the articles there just wasn't any spare money to pay debts.

My Father 1915

Our Bet was the one who always went to the shops for Mam or Auntie Jule. She wouldn't forget and new what to buy, she'd always run and I'd watch her running up Tredegar St to the shops. Her heels always seemed to be kicking her bum. She would be very quick and reliable.

Our Aunt Julie, who lived opposite us, on a Monday dinner time would send one of us to the Pawn shop 'Sollies' in Bute Terrace to pawn a couple of woollen blankets until Friday evening, when her sons would be paid. One of us would go back to the pawn shop with the pawn ticket and money to get the blankets back. She'd pay a sum for lending the money for 5 days. My Mam would be upset by this, she would never do it but people would think that she was sending us to the pawn shop. Auntie Julie would also send me or Dan to the Bridgewater pub to buy two flagons of bitter beer for her to drink. My Mam also hated that but wouldn't say anything, she was a quiet natured lovely woman.

Our Tommy was the only one to have a bike and Mam got that on the new thing Halfords brought out, you can buy only a bike but pay 2/6 D regularly every week or they'd reclaim it back even if you missed one week. He needed to go to work at Robinson and Davids timber merchants in East Moors Rd and Tom wouldn't let anyone touch that bike. He'd be forever cleaning it. He was the only one of us to have money box to save pennies and halfpennies in. Dan used to steal a halfpenny and Tom knew as he was always counting it up and Dan would have to give it back.

My sister Margaret was 11 ½ year older than me so in my mind she was an adult. She worked in Fulton Dunlop's Brewery in Working St, an archwayed building opposite the old Library. She also worked behind the counter in Fultons Wine Shop on the corner of St John's Square. She married Jack Shorter before the war in 1936 and they lived in rooms in Avondale Crescent Grangetown. I often walked down from Rodney St to visit her and Jack. Year later she had a council house on the Gabalfa estate where she now still lives. They had two lovely children John in 1942 and Margarette in 1944.

She used to write me when I was abroad for three and a half years, I looked forward to her letters. Mam always wrote regular letters to me and she would also send parcels of 200 Woodbines now and again. They cost quite a bit to send to me. As I said Jack was in lodgings in London during the war, he may just have been in the Forces as he was away all the time. He tried to get into the Forces with the rest of us but he was more important repairing bombed buildings in war torn London. Margaret must have felt lonely like most Forces wives.

When we brothers came home on leave on most occasions Jack was in there in the Salutation pub. On one occasion me and Jack went for a few to the Salu' (The Salutation), it was very windy when we were walking back to Rodney St at about 10.30 pm when a gust of wind blew Jack's Trilby from his head and we chased after it, the blackout was on.. He found his Trilby and it wasn't until Mag saw him with it on in our kitchen when she screamed "that's not your Trilby". He had only caught an old Greeks hat instead of his own.

After the war in 1953-4, I often used to call at her house on Gabalfa Avenue for a cup of tea at any time of day if I was working in the area on fixing gates and railings and balustrades. We would have a good chat. She then started working part time at Batemans grocery store and I'd be lucky to catch her in after that.

CHAPTER 2
TEENAGE YEARS

I left school at the start of the Christmas holidays in 1936. I found a job advertised on a board outside a building in Charles Street. It was Carter's printing works and I started at work on the Monday and had finished by Friday evening of the same week. My job was to sweep up the paper cuttings from the cutting machines and put it into a big bag. Then I'd pull down a lever, with all my strength of two arms, and tie it tight with wire, that was then called a paper bail. They had a big heavy hand cart that would be loaded up with the packets of typing paper and I would have to push it as far away as, the bottom of, Cathedral Rd. The truck often tipped up with all the paper spilling onto the road. By the time Friday came I'd had enough and with my pay for the week, seven shillings, in today's money that would be 35 pence, I left.

My next job was a van boy with the swift parcel delivery service, often I would go all over the valleys but I enjoyed working with this small firm. I used to go in the car, a sun beam, it was an open top, a beautiful car and also very powerful. My boss had to use cars because he could not get the licence for vans to carry goods, the railway people objected, which stopped him expanding the business. I was transferred to the valleys paper delivery run which meant I started work at three o' clock in the morning. I loaded up our van with one hundredweight bundles of newspapers and parcels and delivered the newspapers to shops all over the Rhondda valleys. In the winter snow was terrible, we wouldn't return to our depot until about five o'clock in the evening. This was all for eight shillings a week. I did that for a year then I was with the horse-drawn vans collecting parcels from warehouses and from the centre of Cardiff for delivery outside the

Cardiff area. I really enjoyed it, until the firm was bought out by Pickfords and then by the railway.

My next job was in Marks and Spencer's as a stockroom man. That meant I would take clothes, all sorts of types of clothes, shirts, underwear, etc. in the four wheeled basket skip to different counters. The stockroom was on the top floor so I would have to use the lift. I stayed in Marks and Spencer's till I was called up, in January 1942.

At first I was very shy but soon realised there was no need to be like that (it took a few months). I made friends with the other young men working in Marks and Spencer's. Ron Seaward served the cake and bread and Len Davies and Ron Corbett served the fruit and veg, and Howard Evans served the fresh meats. Some of us, Howard Evans Ron Seaward and me would go to the Regency dance hall at Mardy St Grangetown. With the exception of Len Davies none of us could dance. We would go to the Neville public house nearby and have a pint of beer (and it was horrible) and then we would ask the girls to go on the floor with us, so we did enjoy it.

CHAPTER 3
THE WAR BEGAN

At that time, in the war, we used to go fire watching at Marks and Spencer's, if the air raid sirens sounded in the day, which it often did. The shop was cleared of shoppers by us, we would then go on to the roof to watch and ensure no incendiary bombs dropped on to the building. I liked the night shift best of all as we would have the store to ourselves. Cardiff had quite a few air raids from the German bombers both the day and night.

One evening, I was in the Central cinema with my mother when the big Screen caught fire at the back. Then we heard the air raid siren going. There was a panic everyone started to move rush towards the exit I stopped my mother and made her wait until the rush died down. She wanted to go so I had to go with her. When we got to the roadside a lot of buildings were on fire around us and it was as bright as daylight. We could hear the bombers and the Ack, Ack guns firing at them, and see search lights up in the sky. Shrapnel was falling all round us, we could hear it the bouncing on the roofs and on the pavements. My poor mother was rushing home as fast as we could go without tripping over sand bags in the street. She was holding her black straw hat on her head thinking that it would stop the shrapnel from piercing the head. When we got to the house we would go under the stairs in case the house collapsed. That was the safest and only place to go. Sheila, Bet and Alice had gone to Aunt Julie's cellar across the street but my mother wanted to stay in our house.

My brother Tom was in the Territorial Army before the war and was away in camp when war was declared on September 3rd 1939. He didn't come home but had to stay and go into the army, the signal corpse. John, who was in London, was then called back into the Welsh Guards. He was sent to France and ended up in the Dunkirk escape. Danny went to Burma in the artillery. Alice's husband Rob Stratford went to Libya in the tank corps. Bet married Len price who went to the Far East and was then taken prisoner of war for three and a half years. He was in the artillery corps, our Mary's husband John went into the pioneer Corps and our Cissys' husband, Jack in Swansea, went to Crete and Libya in the artillery corps. Our Mags' husband Jack was classed as unfit because he had a deformed ankle, from childhood. As he was a brick layer he was sent to London rebuilding bombed buildings.

Of course, I went to Algiers, Tunisia and Italy as an infantry man, like my brother John who was also in the infantry. My mother had a great deal of worry during the war, with four sons' away and four sons' in-law also in the army. It must have been a very worrying five years for her. Our sister Betty was worried sick as for three years she didn't know anything about her husband Len. The Japanese wouldn't allow the prisoners of war to send any letters to their relations in Britain. She saw his name in the morning paper three years after he was captured so she knew then that he was alive, they had only got married just before he was sent abroad in 1941. Our Tom went to Italy in North Africa in 1944 or 1945 at the end. I had my medical examination when I was 18 years old in 1941 and was passed as A1. That meant I was fit for service and I was expecting to be called into the force at anytime.

The war didn't look too good for Britain, the Germans and Japanese were winning every battle in the war. Luckily the Germans didn't invade Britain after France fell, as we didn't have anything to stop them taking over our country. The Germans captured all of the countries in Europe and wanted to capture, firstly, Russia and then they would be able to land Britain, meaning that we would all have been slaves. They didn't think we were worth worrying about at that time, thank God.

I was awoken one morning by my mother, she had a brown letter in her hand. She said "Oh My God they've put you in the foot sloggers", which meant I was to report to the Welsh Regiment. This was in the Maindy area of Cardiff and was the Welsh Regiment headquarters, the Welsh regiment is of course infantry, or foot sloggers. I had to report to Aylesham in Norfolk on January 14th 1942. Also enclosed with the letter were the rail tickets. I'd didn't know what she meant by foot sloggers but I soon found out.

Six months before, I had gone to the RAF recruiting offices in Frederic Street and said to the chap behind the desk that I would like a be in the RAF. He told me that they had plenty of vacancies for men and I replied that this was good and asked what I would be doing. He said we are always looking for rear gunners in the aircraft. Fortunately I had the sense to realise how dangerous that would be, I turned down his offer and said I would rather be on the ground. (I saw what happened to rear gunners when I was guarding the air fields in Norfolk, they would sweep up the remains of the poor rear gunners, into a bag.)

I enjoyed my last Christmas at home knowing I would be leaving on January 14. The days just flew by but I didn't worry about going because all my mates in my age group were being called up. My mates from Marks and Spencer's were all going into the RAF. The reason I was sent into the army must have been because I was more physically developed than a lot of the RAF personnel. Army service, especially infantry, required you to be very strong in the body to survive. I thought I was fit, at just 10 stone 7 pounds with no fat.

CHAPTER 4
LEAVING HOME

I woke to the silence of snow falling in the dark of early morning. My nose was cold in the still air of my bedroom. In contrast I was warm, wrapped in the bedclothes of my youth, protected from all harm and surrounded by the security of my mother four brothers and four sisters.

It was good to feel this way and in time to come I would realise how much I had, and lost, as I was thrown into life, raw and bitter but still with the loving memories of my childhood and strength of character which would take me through the turmoil ahead of me.

As I lay there daring myself to jump out from the warmth of my bed into the cold of my room, I could here the clatter of the kettle and saucepan as my mother prepared a porridge breakfast for me, for the first time in my life I was leaving home. It was 4.30 am and I lay there exited but fearful, like the first unaided leap into water, scared and in trepidation of what was to come, as I would leave today, to go to war.

It was the 14th Jan 1942 and at 5.30 a.m. I kissed my heartbroken mother goodbye on the doorstep of our home at number 7 Rodney St Cardiff. The snow had settled on the pavement outside my house and waiting for me was Mike Geen who lived in Adam St. just a stones throw away. His wife was with him.

We were going to the same unit in the Army, the 18th battalion of the Welsh Regiment, stationed in Norfolk. In my nineteen years of life I had never left Cardiff and had no comprehension of what this meant, other than I would be a long way from home. This point was smothered by the youthful compulsion to explore every opportunity to its extreme even forgoing the pain of leaving family and home, the value of which would only become apparent with the hindsight of experience.

We boarded the 6.15 a.m. train from Cardiff General Station with many other recruits. There was laughter, noise, shouts and goodbye's. As the train pulled away I am sure they were all feeling the same fear and held the same thoughts as I. These were all kept hidden as we all endeavoured to show how strong we were to hold no such feelings.

As the journey continued past snow covered hills the cargo of men quietened, each reflecting on the reality of their lives. My heart was heavy, but Mam had given me sandwiches and biscuits to eat on the journey with which I consoled myself. Mike Geen had nothing so I shared my only consolation with my companion.

The train pulled to a halt at 12 noon in London. We gathered our rucksacks and stepped off into utter confusion. It was full of people rushing places with an urgency, and tunnel vision similar to the scatter of cornered rats. We were soon directed by a couple of military police to tube station where we were marshalled onto another train and then onward to a special train to Norfolk. There must have been a thousand or more men on board' enough to make a battalion strength for training. This took us directly to Norwich where we were met by Sergeants and Corporals from the Welsh regiment, and loaded into separate lorries destined for different units in various villages.

Mike and I were sent to Aylesham a small village 15 miles from Norwich. After fifteen hours of travelling we were cold confused and hungry. It was 9.00 p.m. and we were marched into a cold mess room where a barely cooked meal was awaiting the 100 men who had undergone a similar experience to ourselves. We ate the pitiful offerings and in hope that breakfast would be more substantial thirty of us were taken to sleep and billet above a barn behind a pub called The Red Lion.

We were all supplied with a cameos sack, six foot by three foot, and instructed to go into the barn below and fill it with straw. At this early stage the instincts of self preservation were taking hold and I filled the sack with as much straw as could be compressed into it. This caused it to become round. When I came to sleep on it, in my designated sleeping area, I rolled off it. This continued all night and for as many nights as it took to flatten under my persevering weight. In the first nights men would cry in the loneliness of the dark feeling lost and abandoned.

At 6 a.m. the next morning we were paraded outside and marched to the drill hall (dinner hall) about half a mile away for breakfast. The rest of day was spent collecting our Khaki uniform and Glengarry hat, also two pairs of heavily studded boots, one pair of black canvas shoes, two pairs of socks, vests, shirts under pants, an overcoat, woollen gloves and grey denim blouse and trousers for mucky training.

Then we were asked for our personnel details, even though it had been done months ago. We were given a pay book, my weekly pay and inoculations were eventually entered into this book. We were paid two shillings and sixpence a day that worked out at seventeen shillings and six a week. I had made an order for ten shillings a week to be stopped from my pay and sent to my mother. As a result she would be classed as my dependant, and if I was killed in action she would get a small pension, otherwise she could claim nothing. Seventeen shillings and sixpence is worth eighty-seven pence of today's money.

In the evening of the same day we all had to report to the drill hall for inoculations in our left arm. I cannot recall what they were for. The number of big strong men who fainted just looking at the man in front of them having the needle injected amazed me. At this point we had all received army regulation haircuts.

Each morning we were woken at 6 am and marched half a mile to the mess hall for breakfast. This was always welcome as we were constantly hungry from the exercise and appetite synonymous with early manhood. After breakfast we'd change into gym shorts and vests, issued to us on the second day following our arrival, but we would keep our boots on for the 6 mile jog to follow. These were made for war, strong but heavy and the further we ran the heavier they became. After the first week we were just about exhausted and the arrival of plimsolls did much to boost our morale. During the day we would learn how to drill, march, fire a rifle, bayonet charge and the like.

The village of Aylesham was just one main street with very small side turnings, but just a country village until the Army came. The surrounding area was ideal for Infantry training, marshlands and woods, hence the reason for choosing it.

We were in training for about three months, then given one week's leave to go home in uniform. We were then sent to different Company's in the Battalion. I believe the Company's were A, B, C, D and Headquarters Company. We were all allotted to different airfields that were to be protected by your Company in the case of German Paratroopers landing and capturing for their own planes to land.

CHAPTER 5
REVENGE OR ACCIDENT

Each company had four Platoons of thirty men and each Platoon had three sections of ten men. The platoons were controlled by a Sergeant, who had three stripes. The Sections were controlled by a corporal, who had two stripes, and a Lance Corporal, who had one stripe. Every third day a Platoon would be on standby duty. This meant the thirty men and sergeant would parade at first light and then spread out around the side of the Airfield to keep a look out in case Germans invaded. Dawn in summer would be about 3.30 am to 4.30 am and last light of day was at 12 midnight to 1 a.m.

It would be awfully cold and lonely in those lanes at 3.30 a.m., half asleep and on your own. In your rifle would be a bullet already to fire (just in case). At 4.30 a.m. the sergeant would blow a whistle and we'd all run back to where he was. He would march us back near to our Nissan huts, where we slept, line us up and tell us to work the rifle bolts, to eject the bullet and then press the trigger to make sure there were no more bullets in the rifle. We all pressed the triggers and there was a single shot fired. Someone had fired a round off but no one new who it was. The sergeant put his nose to each riffle to sense the offending barrel. When he reached mine he screamed, "LEE you're the culprit".

I was promptly marched by two men, at the double, to the guard room and locked in a cell with only a hard wooden bed to lie on. I fell asleep and pleasantly dreamed till the guards woke me at 8.00 am. I was marched before the commanding officer at 9.00 am and given 7 days confined to barracks (we didn't go anywhere in any case). I was also ordered to be on parade at 6.00 am every morning to dig the garden in front of the office, followed at the end of the day by the same punishment.

Needless to say the young recruits were taken advantage of by some of the older soldiers. A corporal in my section was such a person he was a half-caste from Adam street, Cardiff. I found that a brand new pair of my army issue grey socks were stolen I then noticed this corporal darning the heel of a new pair of socks, my socks. I told him that I thought that he had stolen my socks, he denied it and I couldn't prove that they were mine. I really disliked him and I hoped that I could get my own back.

Well, one day, we were on Manoeuvres running across this field with our bayonets fixed on the end of our rifles. We were on a mock battle field that involved us running towards a row of bushes with a stream behind it. The corporal was leading and shouting "Follow me". Well I was right behind him with my 18" bayonet attached to my rifle. We had to jump over the stream, he jumped and I followed. There staring me in the face was my revenge, somehow I tripped and the end point of my bayonet went about an inch into the cheek of his bottom. He lay screaming on the grass and a brigadier, an officer watching, said to the corporal "Maybe you haven't been treating this soldier properly". I never had any more trouble with that corporal or any others after that episode.

CHAPTER 6
FEAR AND TRAINING

There were some characters who wanted to work their ticket out. One from North Wales said he couldn't speak English, but we knew he could, so when we were given orders on the parade ground he wouldn't obey. He would plead he couldn't understand the language and upset the Corporal who would send him off the parade ground. He also used to wet his bed, he'd stink of urine. The medical officer made him sleep in the guard room and the guard was ordered to wake him up every two hours to urinate. He was also not allowed to drink after 8.00 p.m. but he used to sneak out to the Pub for a few pints. The guards wouldn't bother saying anything resulting in his bed and clothes being soaking and stinking every morning. He eventually got his ticket home.

Others would perforate their ear with a pointed match-stick, and others would swallow a small piece of soap just before going to see the Medical Officer. This would make their heart beat at double the normal rate. Another pretended he couldn't see very well and continued to bump into things as proof. He was sent to have his eyes tested but he would lie to the optician and confuse the test so much that they threw him out. Even so, the same man would quite happily read the newspaper, with the lights out, by the fire light every night. He got his ticket because no Sergeant or Corporal would have him as he wouldn't do anything right. He'd stay in the barrack room sweeping up but he also wouldn't do that properly as he'd leave bits of paper on the floor to prove his disability. The difficulty with all of these was that you had to continue to repeat all the things you faked and that could go on for months. Once you stared to work your ticket it could be a long, long test of nerves!!

The training was hard, over assault courses, as we would run in full kit and carrying rifles weighing nine pounds. Route marches started off at fifteen miles and then after a couple of weeks they lengthened to thirty miles. We had a ten minute stop every hour and marched 120 paces a minute, which was about four or five miles an hour, so a thirty mile route march would take all day. Every time we would stop to rest our burning, throbbing feet it would be very painful to start again. The Medical Officer would examine our feet for blisters and he'd burst them with a sterilised needle. After six months we had two weeks leave of course my mother could not wait to see how I looked and If they were treating me right.

Around August time we were on manoeuvres again, about twenty of us were in the back of this army lorry being taken to where the mock battle would begin. I was sitting at the tail end of a 10 cwt lorry. There were long wooden benches on both sides of the inside of the lorry. The driver of the lorry went around a corner in the country road to fast, he skidded, the end of the lorry smashed against a stone wall. Many of us were thrown out, I landed on the road and came to in hospital. I think it was St. Andrews hospital, Norwich. My left elbow was split on the radius, my face was all scraped and my left knee was damaged. I was unconscious for twenty hours or so. They put my arm in plaster and after a week in hospital I was sent to a convalescent home a big manor house taken over by the army. I made the most of this especially the food and visits to the apple and pear orchards. I was there about a month or so, I didn't let my mother know of this incident as it would have worried her too much. If I had been a little bit crafty I could have said that my elbow was giving me pain and I would have been down graded from A1 (fit) to a lower grade. I would have been out of the infantry, discharged, but I was young and fit so just carried on as before.

Mike Geen and I learnt to be drivers. Mike unfortunately failed but we were taught to drive a Brenn gun carrier, a small armoured tracked vehicle. The damage I did learning is still unaccounted for but there were a few hedges that were worse off for the experience. I never actually became a driver but I was able to claim a driving licence, after the war, without a driving test. Around this time I was admitted to hospital at Cottersham aerodrome for three weeks with acute bronchitis due to being wet in the marshes of Norfolk in training.

Around the end of September I ended up in hospital again when a lorry crashed into the back of ours. We were on a mock battle again when the lorry taking us to the assembly point stopped and the lorry behind ran into the back of us. A few of us were thrown out onto the ground. I fell on my back and couldn't move for the pain. It was late at night so I was taken to an RAF first aid post overnight. The next day I was taken to hospital for an examination and X rays. They found that the muscles alongside the left of my spine had been torn, disabling movement. After a week there I was taken to a convalescent home for four weeks. Our battalion was moved to a different airfield in Norfolk and in December we were billeted in closed down hotels on the Gromer sea front. It was cold and deserted.

That is a brief resume of my training period. A time that made men of boys and abruptly finished my childhood days which were now a long and distant memory, only to be called upon in times of desperation.

CHAPTER 7
ABROAD FOR THE FIRST TIME

It was rumoured that we were to be sent abroad, to India, for the benefit of German spies. We were issued with tropical type clothes and taken by train to Southampton. We embarked from Southampton around March 1943 on the troopship cruiser "SS Franconia". It had been a passenger cruise ship in peace times (an ex Cunard Star Passenger Liner) and had been altered to carry two thousand troops, but there were five thousand on board. When she sailed you can imagine the mess with the extra lot of men crowded below deck, the toilets always over flowing. The good thing about all of that was that I was never sea sick. All around me were sea sick men, for four or five days, so I ate all of the food. The food was freshly cooked on board, the bread was beautiful, I was the only one on my table who wasn't sea sick and so I ate their rations as well for about 4 days. As I recall we were six weeks getting to Algiers it seemed a long time. The convoy pretended to go to India to confuse any U-boats waiting for us on the way to India. This probably extended the journey somewhat.

Algiers looked like a breath of fresh air as we entered harbour. As we pulled alongside the wharf we could smell the hundreds of little Arab boys shouting up to us begging for money, cigarettes or anything else we cared to throw them.

When we landed in Algiers we had to march seven miles so to a mosquito ridden swamp like camp. We handed in our kit of Indian clothes and were issued with short trousers and shirt to suit the heat. We were warned not to go to Algiers because it would be perilous on the road back in the dark. Of course there are always some who simply must try it, three soldiers' bodies were found stripped of all clothing in ditches the next morning. Arabs were regarded as scum, muggers who were cowardly, sly cut-throats.

We were eight men to a tent and of course no beds just sleeping on your ground sheet on the hard earth. In the evening me and my mates went to the camp canteen, a big Nissan hut that sold wine in round tin containers (old cigarette tins). Well, we thought it was wine but we found out too late. We were later to find out that it was cognac, and very strong at that. All I remember is that we were singing sentimental songs with tears running down our cheeks by the end of the night.

The last thing I remember was being thrown out at stop tap and talking to a commando, who was wearing head bandages, asking him what it was like up at the front line in Tunisia. The next thing I saw was the stars in the sky and wondering to myself what I was doing lying on my back in the bushes looking up at the stars. I tried to turn over to get up, but couldn't move any part of my body, it was very frightening. I was thinking clearly, but my body was incapable of movement. Then I saw a lantern and heard someone say "Here's another one", and they dragged me through the bushes and flung me into my tent. I was up most of the night hanging on to the front tent pole on my knees, vomiting, For days afterwards I felt drunk when only drinking tea or water. I was always very wary of drinking any strange drinks after wards and even to this day I have never again been as drunk as that.

After about a week we were marched to a railway siding and put into cattle vans, supposed to hold sixteen soldiers but forty-five of us were jammed in. We had no room to lie down or move. With forty-five in the cattle van it was like an oven during the day and a fridge at night. We would fight to get by the door in the day then try to get at the back during the night, to keep out of the draft.

It took us over a week to get near to Tunisia, where the battle front was, eventually arriving at a place called Phillipville. We disembarked from the train and marched to our new camp, made on a hill outside the town. Unknown to us, they were to break us up as the eighteenth battalion Welsh regiment, into smaller groups. We would be used to fill up units, in the front line, that were short of men. This was due to the killing by the German army in Tunisia only a couple of days away from where we were camping.

Many of my mates and me volunteered to join the light Infantry. We were part of the 46th Canadian division in the American first army. Although it was called the American first army there appeared to be more British soldiers than Americans in it. So, I chose to join the light infantry, in fact the only units open to go into were light infantry (the Welsh regiment was heavy in infantry). In the light infantry you march 160 paces to the minute, about seven miles an hour. In the heavy infantry it was 120 paces to the minute which was four miles an hour. So it was nearly double marching time, a terrible strain on the back muscles of the legs, especially in the hot climate we were in, it was like learning to march all over again.

Now, apart from the flies and sunburn we had more serious things to worry about, no one liked the thought of going into the front line. We joined our new infantry company just outside Tunisia. The

German army were still fighting to hold onto that area but luckily for us they gave in, surrendered, after we had been in the front line a fortnight. It was bad enough even for that short time and quite a few were wounded. Even so I was relieved and happy.

CHAPTER 8
THE ATLAS MOUNTAINS

For the next month or two my company was guarding thousands of prisoners of war, Germans and Italians in different concentration camps in Tunisia. We were then back on the railway to Algeria for more training. We were transported all the way back down the railway line to just outside Algiers to a place called Blida, about twenty or thirty miles from Algiers. We were camped in an area that was flat for as far as the eye could see except to the left which was the foot of the Atlas mountains. The area was flat country to train for the coming battle in Italy, also as we were at the bottom of the Atlas Mountains it was similar to the mountains in Italy. It wasn't a bad camp, plenty of room, with eight men to each tent, sleeping on the floor of course. The flies were infinite. Even trying to write a letter home was a chore as the flies would be never ceasing to reach the sweat on my face.

All we were allowed, in water rations, was one pint of water a day, brought to our camp by water wagons. We used to shave and wash our bodies in just that pint of water in our tin mugs. We had a pint of tea at breakfast and at tea time there was no more water to have anywhere. If we wanted to drink the pint of water we had to put two tablets in it to purify it. It was full of small worms, and could cause you to develop dysentery and other diseases. Our toilet was a deep pit with a pole about twelve feet long for us to balance on. My Mam had given me a plastic crucifix to wear around my neck with my two identity discs. The cross had somehow got broken and a pointed piece stuck into my chest. It eventually became infected causing large boils over my chest and back which would burst oozing blood and pus over my shirt and vest. The medical officer couldn't cure it due to the heat and infectious air. They would not heal in that climate and I still carry the scars on my back and chest to this day.

A new young 2nd Lieutenant officer came from England to join our unit. He was full of his own self importance and thought he was a tough guy, in the end he showed how much of a coward he was.

Of all the stupid things: He led our Company, of about a hundred men, to climb the Atlas mountains to practice climbing and mock battles. He marched us to the top of Atlas Mountain in the hottest part of the day; starting at 9.00 am. As we were light infantry we marched fast, 160 paces per minute. We were only trained to march in the heavy infantry which is 120 paces a minute, quite slow compared to the light infantry. Although we were fit men, altering our march to a faster speed made our leg muscles ache and exhausted us quickly.

At the foot of the road leading to the top of the mountain we were told not to drink until we were ordered. This was because there was no water until we reached the camp at the top of the mountain. However, every time we were told to stop for a rest we would have to drink out of necessity. By the time we were three quarters of the way up we had exhausted our water supplies and to keep, our mouths moist we had to put a pebble in our mouths to generate saliva. We were in a sorry state, sweating out the moisture from our bodies, our heads were aching and the higher we got the harder breathing became. It took us about four hours to reach the top, we were just about crazed for water, and we were ignoring his orders because we felt he had done the wrong thing with us.

We all just sat in the shade of the hill, with our tongues partly swollen, refusing to budge an inch unless we had a drink. There was a dry river bed nearby and a few of us started to dig for water using our army knifes but no luck. Then someone said we had a tin of soup in our rations in our pack. Without thinking we made holes in the top of the tins and drank them. We forgot that it contained salt and it made us even more thirsty.

From the Back Streets to the Front Line

Water Falls at Blida (Atlas Mountains)

> **CORRESPONDANCE**
> I was stationed at Blida, not far from Algiers (30 miles) North Africa 1943
> Dad
>
> **ADRESSE**
> This scene is on the top of the Atlas Mountains. I drank from this waterfall, our company were very grateful for this water. 16th Battalion Durham Light Infantry 1943

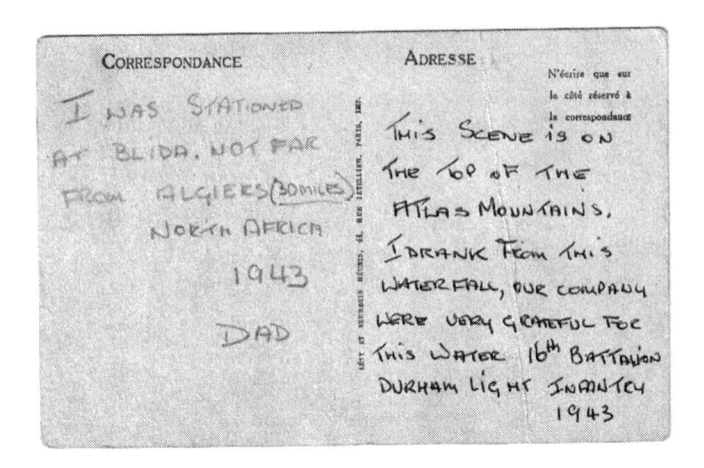

After some time a little Arab shepherd boy came by with his herd of goats. Someone asked where there was water he pointed up the road and we all ran to get some. The officer tried to make us march to get it, but no one took any notice of him, we just ran past him and around the bend where we soon came to a beautiful small waterfall with a pool at the bottom. We first drank but not too much as we knew we would get Colic if we drank too much at first. When we drank the water we put no tablets in to purify it. We were so desperate and thirsty, and being thirsty is a terrible feeling, that we gulped the water but not to fast as we knew we would get colic, and that causes terrible pains in the stomach.

We were all waiting for our pint of tea that the cook had ready resting on the stoves around the fire when he knocked it over and it all ran out onto the ground. He just saved about a third of it by lifting the big cauldron up. The men were so angry he had to run away, up the hill because they would have killed him, we really wanted that tea.

We were three days on those mountains pretending we were in Italy fighting the Germans. Real ammunition was being used so you made sure you kept your body down low in the bushes, the mosquitoes as usual were lively, every night there were hoards of them in Africa. We would sleep where we could, on one occasion I made up my sleeping position on the side of the mountain and when I awoke I looked around and down below was nothing but white clouds. The Sun was just starting to come up and the rays of the Sun shone far away but lit up all the clouds below me. It looked like heaven and so peaceful. When the Sun did come up it dispersed the clouds (that was one or two hours later) then one could see for miles and miles across the landscape below.

We descended by another route and in contrast to the one we had used when ascending it was like a nice walk. We passed a large forest and were told that the monkeys in it had no tails and that it was the only place in the world that they lived. I do not know whether that was true. When we reached the bottom we had to walk through a French owned vineyard. An officer warned us not to touch of the grapes, which was stupid of him. We took what we could reach as we marched through but he saw few of the men eating the grapes and he reported them to the commanding officer. He then fined them an amount of money. No one liked the young officer, he was not one of us.

We stayed on the Blida Plains training before the invasion of Italy. We would practise landing on the beaches at night or we would practise stopping other troops from landing.

CHAPTER 9
BLIDA AND THE BIZERTA EXCURSION

Eventually we marched to the railway depot and once again we were jammed into cattle box van. The trains would travel very slow and there was only a single track. If another train came from the opposite direction then one of them would have to pull into a siding to allow the other to pass. We could run faster than these trains could travel. We were going back to Tunisia to a little sea port village called Bizerta, we had to wait nearby in the Mountains till an invasion force of thousands had assembled. We still trained invading beaches and hills.

In our platoon of thirty men there were three lads from Liverpool. They were inseparable and together they were afraid of no one or nothing. Because the trains would be going so slow and take so long they got bored. They climbed out on top of the cattle van and played follow the leader. The leader of the three was called John and he was a tough fellow. He took the lead jumping from one roof to the other. He fell in between two vans and fell on to the rails his left leg was run over by the wheel and his body was on the other side of the track. His leg was dragged by the wheel. He was dragged bumping on every sleeper for work half a mile and till one of his friends ran along the train to the front where the officers were. They stopped the train and the Medical Officer cut through his knee and threw the leg in a ditch. The man was screaming don't cut my leg off, but it had to be done.

When in camp we would have a cooked dinner every day but no potatoes, these had to be paid for. We always had corned beef to keep us going. When out of camp as we were now, travelling on a train, we would have a tin of corn beef and a packet of rock hard biscuits every day. We didn't have any bread for over six months just hard biscuits, however the officers would have bread. We were always so hungry, I even tried eating unripe figs from a tree growing nearby, I even ate grass. It's so hard to believe when I look back on those horrible days. All the discomfort and pain we went through can't be explained in detail, such as the extreme heat when marching 160 paces to the minute just try it. Your head aches something terrible.

We had to march about six or seven miles to join thousands of British troops all lined up by the side of the road leading to Tunis. This was because Churchill and Montgomery were riding through on a victory parade a week or two after Tunis was captured by the British (although we were in the first American army). We stood there in the blazing sun for one hour or more, our tongues started to swell because we had drunk all our water getting there. We were told to dismiss and we all ran to a well in the yard of an Arabs house. Our Sergeant Major came and drove us away with a big stick, some corporals came to help him for he knew we would be ill after drinking at the water. The filthy Arabs had been used to it all of their lives.

So we had to do without water until we marched back to our camp, but on the way back to the camp we passed near the cost and lovely isolated beaches. We shouted to our sergeant in charge" How about a swim". We came to a beach that was hidden by a small forest and he directed us on to the beach and then told us to strip off and swim. We were in that beautiful water in no time and naked, it was great.

Miles out to sea was a convoy of ships waiting to go in to Tunis to unload. My mate Ernie Chamberlain and I swam out of our depth a few hundred yards from the beach. Then I saw this black tapered shape bobbing and moving towards us. "Sharks" I shouted and I started to swim as fast as Tarzan, or faster. There are sharks in that the area of the sea. Ernie followed but was way behind me. When I could feel the bottom of the sea I looked back. Ernie was calling and shouting that it's only a broken boat front. We never went out so far after that fright. Swimming made us all the more thirsty.

We slept in two man tents. When we laid our blankets on the floor in the evening we made sure there were no insects or crawlies there, especially one big black beetle that could bite you. It had a back leg, only on, and it could jump three or four feet in the air. You can imagine why we didn't want that thing in the tent. When we first put the tent up we didn't know of these insects. In the middle of the night we felt a few of them walking or crawling over us. We jumped up and took the tent down in panic as did a lot of the blokes that night. The Arabs were always hanging around camp scrounging anything. They would buy cigarettes, tea and sugar, etc. Some clever fellows would sell the Arabs a packet of tea or two. It would be old used tea leaves, dried and put back into the packet and a little bit of new tea placed on top which the Arabs would want to see. They'd come back the next day playing hell but wouldn't get any money back. The Arabs were very cunning especially at night.

In the Blider camp we had six men to a tent, as I said, we would lie on the floor on blankets and a blanket over us. The Arab boys would crawl under the front of the tent and tickle the nearest man's ear with a feather. This would make him roll of over to that side and the boy would fold the blanket in to your back and then tickle your other ear. You would roll back off the blanket. He would roll the blanket push it out of the tent and the then take the blanket slowly from the top covering you and off he'd go with any other stuff he could take.

CHAPTER 10
SOLERNO AND THE FRONT LINE

Thousands of troops assembled on a hill outside the embarkation port of Bizerta. This was not far from Tunis and at night the German air planes would come to fire on us and bomb us. We had plenty of anti-aircraft guns firing at them and brought a couple down. The sky would be covered in tracer bullets and shells. Tracers are bullets made to emanate light in the dark, every fifth round would be a tracer, you would know where the bullets were going then.

Four others and I had terrible stomach pains. We were taken to an American field hospital a mile or so away. We had a form of dysentery which was very uncomfortable. We were put to bed and we stayed there for three or four days. When we were discharged our company and everyone else had gone. They had invaded Italy at Solerno beach and we were told it was a massacre. The Germans were waiting for our troops to land, and they nearly wiped them out. A lot of my company were killed.

The five of us were taken to Solerno by Americans in a small gun boat. We had to wade ashore to the transit and advise the officer of who we were and where our company was. This was so we could follow them and join them. I had to wait in the transit camp until the position of my unit was known. It took a few more days. I saw one very young curly haired boy from my platoon walking around. I called him and he was so glad to see me he was crying. He said he deserted when the firing and killing got too much for him, he'd just dropped his rifle, ran and hid. Now, he asked me what he could do because he could be shot for deserting in the face of the enemy.

The firing and killing around him and the mortars and shells exploding meant he just lost control and ran and hid in a hedge until his unit moved away and then he realised that what he had done meant a long imprisonment for deserting. So, I said stay with me and when I am told to go into a vehicle to take me to your unit then you can come and say you fell and was knocked unconscious. We had to wait for a few more days in this transit camp until our company was found and we shared a two-man bivouac. The first night we had an electric storm. The wind and rain was terrible and we could see great balls of fire on the mountain tops, I assume these were bolts of lightening. The American ships anchored in the nearby bay were tossed up and down on big waves, a couple broke loose from their anchors and there was all hell let loose. The wind was so powerful it blew our tent away into the sky and we just ran under the closest vehicle.

The sun came out in the morning and we dried all of our clothes in no time at all. Eventually I was told a small army core, just four men, would take me back to my unit so I then said that there was one more to take and they said OK let's go. Harry got in by me along with two other soldiers and we were soon climbing up the mountain pass. After about an hour mortars and machine guns were firing on us, the car fell into a ditch and the soldiers and driver were killed. Harry was hit on the top of his right arm and he was screaming like a stuck pig. I told him to shut up and we crawled through the filthy water for quarter of an hour or so then we hid in a forest. I took his coat off him and he was bleeding bad so I used his emergency dressing which every soldier has on the top of his left trouser leg. The pocket is stitched up so I cut the thread and applied the field dressing to his wound. Now, where to go?, there were still Germans in the area. We walked through the woods to the next valley and hid in a small cave but some lads saw us and ran away shouting "Englessi, Englessi" in Italian. We could not go any further so we just waited for someone to come, after two hours I could hear someone shouting to us in English, as a matter of fact with a Welsh twang to it. I shouted back, he said "I'm coming into the cave so don't shoot", I said "OK come in". a young man about 22 years old stood up and walked up to us, he said he was from Wales born and bread in the Rhonda Porth town as a fact. He said he had come here before the war with Italy was declared, for a visit to his Father's family who lived in the village near by and couldn't return to Britain until the war ended. He brought us food and water for three days, he also gave us some blankets.

We could get plenty of tree wood for a fire and I had my army mess tins in my small pack so we could eat hot soup now and again. On the third day he came to tell us there was a Fascist group looking for British soldiers in the area so he took us, at night, to another cave which he said goes right up a tunnel to the top of the mountain. He gave me a torch and said I would be safer going up this tunnel to get into the other valley, so we thanked him and I said I would call to see him after the war in his home town of Porth. We could see men with shotguns coming up the mountain so I said to Harry "let's go quick, these Fascists would shoot at us or catch us and hand us over to the Germans". We walked to the back of the cave and saw this tunnel leading us to the top of this shaft, it looked very high up and we started to climb straight away. About twenty feet up there was a ledge and this ledge was a black bear, asleep. I put my bayonet on the end of my rifle (a soldier always has the same rifle for the time he is in the army and it has a serial number stamped on it so he knows it is his), Harry lost his rifle when he ran away because he wasn't in his right mind. I had to calm Harry down but with his shouting in fear, the bear woke up, growled and moved towards us. Harry scrambled up and away, I kept the bear at bay stabbing it with my bayonet and shinning the torch light in its eyes so it couldn't see what was attacking him so I slowly managed to climb up following Harry who was way up the shaft by now.

We eventually climbed out at the top in pitch blackness, we didn't know where to go but after our eyes were used to the darkness (we didn't use the torch in case it was seen) I saw a small shed and we went in it, then I put the torch on and there was two men asleep on the floor, they jumped up in panic, I calmed them down and they noticed we were British not German. They lit a hurricane lamp and warned us that there were German patrols still in the area and they were behind British front lines and hiding so they would kill us if we saw them. These men were shepherds and they told us to stay in the hut for the rest of the day and they would bring us food and let us know how to reach the British army lines. It was a long day for us but eventually a Partisan came in the evening with food, he could speak a bit of English and said his group of Partisans (freedom fighters) would lead us to safety in the night. They came for us about midnight and it was pouring down with thunder and lightening and a gale to contend with, all the better said the Partisan as the Germans would not be out in this weather, the trouble was Harry and me we didn't have any waterproof clothing only our uniforms, still that was the least of our worries. So off we went, three Partisans, Harry and me, we had scrambled about two miles when a voice shouted "Alt ve is das" (halt who is that), none could speak German so we all ran up another hillside with the German firing at us and just our luck a German patrol was coming down back to their camp. They fired on us, killed one of the Partisans, we fired back at them and saw one of them drop backwards, they stopped firing and kept their heads down and we ran like hell. The Partisans went back to their village and me and Harry ran as fast as we could over the hill and in the distance we could hear and see a lot of gunfire and mortar fire so we kept running until we met some British soldiers on patrol. They nearly shot us, we told their Captain about the German patrol behind and he sent three patrols to attack or capture them. They gave us food and a ten to sleep in until they found our unit. Next day Harry's wound was in a very bad state by now so he had to go to a field hospital further back. His desertion, he didn't say anything about only that he got hit and was left wounded until he met me at the transit camp. There is no way his unit would doubt his word and mine so all's well that ends well. Eventually I caught up with my Company, they had been street fighting on the Naples suburbs, our machine gunner was killed.

CHAPTER 11
THE RESULT OF WAR

Eventually I caught up with my unit. They had been Street fighting, house to house, in Naples. It was terrible and a lot of men had been killed. A Brenn gunner was killed by a sniper (they always shoot at the machine gunners). I spoke to one of the two remaining lads from Liverpool and he said that it had been a nightmare. His mate was shell-shocked and sitting on his own with his mind going through fear of all he had gone through. So, of the three Liverpudlian's who were invincible together there was now only the one on his own. It's terrible what these stupid wars do to young and old people alike.

A group of young soldiers joined us from Britain. It was the first time they had been abroad and been in the army. They didn't know how to operate the Brenn gun, so they sat around in a circle and a corporal showed them how to load and use the gun. He said to one of them "Now you show me how to operate the gun". The lad lay down in front of the gun and pressed the magazine of bullets down into the gun and pressed the trigger pretending to fire on his friend. A stream of bullets came out and killed him stone dead. It happened so quickly, no one moved because of the shock of the gunfire. The poor lad nearly went crazy because he killed his best mate, he was taken away to hospital and most likely was never the same.

We were resting and sleeping in this little farmyard, the hayrack was alive with rats. Close by was a destroyed church, it had once been the village church. We led on the floor with our clothes on and went to sleep. In the middle of the night, a scream of panic woke us up. One of the lads had put his boots on to go to the toilet, and found a rat in his boot. There was panic among all of us because we could hear the rats squeaking, but we had no lights and so, we couldn't see them. We didn't rest well that night.

CHAPTER 12
THE VOLTURNO RIVER

Rumours started that we were going to the front line. We were transported to a village close to the river Volturno. On the other side of the river the Germans were waiting for us to cross over. In my opinion there is no doubt that a German soldier is as good as a British soldier when it comes to fighting. We were told we were going to cross the river Volturno soon.

It was pouring down, cold and dark when a lorry dropped us off a half mile from the river Volturno. We also had a ten man small boat to carry to the river. I was with my company and we were to cross the river and move about half a mile inland which would take us behind the German line. We were then to capture and hold a small flat bridge to enable the tanks to proceed, as the area consisted of large earth mounds everywhere. This flat bridge would allow the tanks to get through and advance.

After carrying the boat a long distance across grass and the like we arrived at the river. We could see it would be impossible to use the boat as the river was over flowing and rushing too fast to try a boat on it. So a volunteer was requested. He had to swim across the river with a rope tied to his waist. When and if he got across he had to tie it to a tree so that we could all cross over. We were soaking wet in any case, but we did eventually get across.

Time was getting on and we should have been in our positions before dawn. The volcano Vesuvius was behind us shooting flames. Eventually we assembled on the opposite bank, ready to go forward when the whole sky above us was lit up by 'Verry Lichts'. The German's got wind of us and fired these 'Verry Lichts' to see what's what, it seemed as though we were in blazing sunlight after it being so dark and rainy. Then, panic set in. 'Run and follow me' shouted our commanding officer. We were then, to make for and run across three open fields towards a wooden gate. We had to get through that gate to able to reach our objective. Alongside the gate was a big hedge and as we approached the hedge a machine gun behind it, opened fire on us. He couldn't see us, but could hear us. His machine gun was just firing in one line, up and down, to keep us down, as I've said before, every fifth bullet was white hot, so he could judge where his bullets were going.

We lay there divided, one half of us to the left of the line of bullets, the other half of us to the right. We were naturally lying down as close to the ground as we could. I looked up, just a bit, and could see the line of bullets just two feet to my right. Then one of the tracers hit the metal part of a fellow's heel, that's how close the bullets were. It bounced off the man's heel right into the throat of the man just in front of me, 'Aargh' he went, and was dead. My head was pressed as far down as possible after that.

How long we were there I can't say, it seemed like hours but I suppose thinking about it, I'd say about 15 minutes. What made us move was the probability of German mortar bombs exploding on us. I could see over to my left these six inch mortar bomb machines, they'd light up when fired, and the frightening noise they'd make, like a big giant vomiting noise.

The first lot of a group of six mortar bombs fell and exploded to our left. Then a group to the right, and if we didn't move, the next lot would be on top of us. Our commanding officer passed the word to move to the gate and over it when he said. That would be when the machine gunner had to stop to put a fresh belt of cartridges in his gun breech. We moved over the gate and the field was all furrows, which meant we had to crawl over and into these furrows, to the top of the field. We had to keep low and very quiet because the mortar bombs could still follow us. We crossed about fort or five fields, not knowing whether there were Germans there or not. It's not a very nice feeling, like going into a lion's cave, not knowing if he's in there.

CHAPTER 13
BRUSH WITH DEATH, THE FIRST TIME

It was still pouring down and my ears were still deafened by the mortar explosions, that was the starting of my ears being damaged in the future. We eventually arrived at our position, right by the small bridge. Our section of ten men was right alongside this bridge there was only a small flat bit of road with a tunnel underneath. We were told to dig our pits and to get down in them, to protect our bodies and to hide ourselves. I decided to dig at the top side of this high mound of grassed earth, my mate, Ernie, wanted to go down the bottom, so we went where we thought best.

I figured if the Germans came and threw their hand grenades over, I'd be first to knock them down the mound. Some bloke came digging with me and we soon got a hole dug out, it was about three feet deep, four feet long and one and a half foot wide. As we finished, I stood on the top of the mound, I forgot dawn was coming up, so that my figure would be outlined to any one watching behind us, such as a German sniper. Then, Bang!. My helmet spun off my head and I dropped into the pit, shaken up, a bullet had struck my helmet and dented it. So, there was a German sniper behind us, there was an Italian farmhouse not too far away.

The corporal for our section said to me "Lee, you and your mate go over to the opposite mound, and dig in at the bottom. Take a Bern machine gun, hand grenades and your rifle, and if Germans come you can fire on them and protect our mound". Well, I thought, that's the most stupid thing I'd heard. So, I told him to get stuffed, and I wouldn't be so bloody daft to go there. He said he'd report me when we got out of the line, "Ay", I said, "If we get out of the line". So he sent two other men, and of course, they were captured.

Our platoon, second Lieutenant, was the same one we had in North Africa and he hid himself under the bridge in the tunnel. A man with a Brenn gun was laying on top the flat bridge, protecting us.

CHAPTER 14
BRUSH WITH DEATH, SECOND TIME

About mid morning, I could here a voice saying "Now come on, Tommy, hand over your guns, and don't try to fight us, just come out of your hole". The next thing we knew, hand grenades were thrown over on top of us, exploding right and left, it was quite a panic. Now to the right of my pit, was another, right by the top of the bridge. I heard a shout, and looked to this pit, and I could see this Lance Corporal picking up a grenade, and throwing it at this German, who was lying behind a Brenn gun. The grenade blew him to bits, the grenades were set with a two or three second fuse.

The German had just started to fire the gun, as the Lance Corporal threw the grenade, and his bullets cut through the Lance Corporals' right ear. I don't know how much of the ear was gone, because he had to go back to the first aid post, half a mile back and he didn't return.

If the Lance corporal hadn't thrown that grenade the German would have killed us as he was above us. We found our machine gunner dead, he had been stabbed through the heart. We threw a grenade back over at the Germans but they laughed at us and threw packets of rough German tobacco cigarettes asking if we would throw some English cigarettes back in exchange. Some of our fools through English cigarettes back. I shouted at the men who threw good cigarettes over, then the Germans threw branches of flowers over, put them on your graves they said and then threw a couple more hand grenades over. One went near the tunnel where are officer was hiding, when it exploded he screamed the place down. "I am wounded" he kept screaming time after time. Then he said fix bayonets, then charge!! he expected us to go charging over the top (crazy). "Charge!!" he kept saying. Now I am in the top hole so I am going to be the first over the top. "No way!!" I shouted "An officer should lead". "Lee" he shouted from inside the tunnel, it's you again causing trouble, I shouted back you lead and we'll follow. "I can't I am wounded" he cried so we all just stayed there. He had a cut above his eyebrow (so it was said).

CHAPTER 15
BRUSH WITH DEATH, THIRD TIME AND THE TOUGH GUY

The sun came out and our clothes started to steam and dry out. The two men sent over to the next mound were gone, captured, all because the officer let a corporal take charge of the unit. It goes to show that you can't rely on anyone, you must look out for yourself. Our officer had gone back to the first aid post. I slid down the mound to have a chat to my mate, Ernie. I sat on the bottom of the mound while he was in his pit and I opened a tin of sardines from my pack to eat for dinner with some hard biscuits.

There was a hedge running in front of this mound and we were behind it. There was a small gap just where I was sitting and the same German sniper had another go at me only with a machine gun this time. The bullets just ripped alongside me and up the mound. I fell, sardines on top of me and into Ernie's pit. I stayed there for a short while until I could smell this other chap's excrement that had run down his leg, we had short trousers on then because it was still warm in the day but we would change into long trouser in the night. This chap was Ernie's pit mate. So that's three times I nearly had it, four times if you count not being at Salerno, so God was definitely looking after me. The sniper's farmhouse was shelled so that was the end of him.

When it was getting towards dusk I was told to collect our sections empty water bottles and go back half mile to a farmhouse, for water. This was our headquarters, so I tied the water bottles together threw them all over my shoulder and crawled along the hedge and down a path. I had been told to go halfway down the path. We were still having trouble with loose Germans, so every bush could hide a German soldier. I came to one bush and a person stepped out and frightened the hell out of me. I swung my riffle to shoot at him and he shouted "No! Lee, it's me". it was Our officer who had gone back from our positions this morning to the first aid post. He pleaded with me to allow him to come back with me, to protect him. He had been too terrified to go back on his own and he had stayed in the bush all day. I reminded him of what he had said to me in North Africa, that we will see who will be the tough guy when we get to the front line. I know, he said, I apologise, but please take me with you. So I made him carry the water bottles all the way to the farmhouse. We were told he was sent back to England and made into an ordinary soldier's rank. Just as well, he would have got a lot of men killed through bad and cowardly leadership.

I was more nervous going back with the full water bottles because they would stop me from using my rifle if needed. They were a heavy weight around my back, but it was o.k., I got back all right and everyone was parched for a drink. Each night someone else would call over for water.

The Germans realised how important this access bridge was to our tanks and tried to dislodge us by firing personnel shells above us. They would explode above us and shrapnel would fall on us. Every day quite a few were wounded by the attacks. It meant we had to stay bent down in our pits to avoid the shrapnel. Just waiting for a piece to hit you was quite nerve racking. Day after day we were stuck there for about a fortnight.

The chap who was in the pit with me was a lot older, about 30 or more and he kept crying most of the time that he should not be there. I told him to shut up or I would throw him out of the pit. He then quietened down. All this crouching down for days on and off made my left knee ache terribly. What I didn't realise was it was damaged badly when I had been thrown out of the lorry in England and now the pressure of bending had made it much worse.

We had a sergeant who went out on his own every night to spy on the Germans, he was a very brave man. I said to him "why do you risk your life every night just for information about where the Germans are". He replied, "Well I haven't got much of a future because I am wanted for bigamy in Britain and when or if I get back to Britain I will be put in jail for several years, so I don't care about my life". One night he didn't come back and that was the end of the sergeant. No one else volunteered to do the same. The mound we were on continued beyond the bridge and tunnel by about fifty feet long. This left our right flank unprotected so at the end of the mound a guard with a Brenn gun and grenades was set up. In the night we would, in turn, go on guard two hours on and four hours off shared by the section. Two men would be on guard every night till dawn next day, no guard was needed during the day.

I'd lie down behind the Brenn gun with it to my shoulder ready to fire in an instance. Ernie, my mate, would be lying alongside me with the hand grenades near his hand and the nights were always wet and freezing cold. With every little movement of a bush out front or to the side, I'd whisper to Ernie, "Look by that bush, something moved", and when you know you can be killed in seconds it put your nerves at a screaming level. After two hours we'd be looking at our watches constantly then another two men would come to take our place. I'd have a job to prise my right hand from the hand grip of the Brenn gun, because, for two hours, I'd held it tightly, ready to fire.

Ernie and me would collapse in a long pit dug nearby and we'd pull our ground sheet over the top and have a couple of, well needed, fags. We'd stay there until needed. We weren't supposed to smoke because if Germans were near, they would smell it and know we were near by. We couldn't have a hot meal for the whole fortnight. We would only eat Bully beef, biscuits, water and now and again we would have sardines.

CHAPTER 16
INTO THE LIONS MOUTH AT SOLERNO

Well, my left knee got so painful when I had to go in the pit, that I told this bloke, in with me, to go to another one so I could straighten the leg out instead of bending it. Eventually, the tanks arrived and assembled in a field behind us, I spoke to a few of the tank drivers. A day or so after that, we were pulled out of that area and went a couple of miles back, to a village and we were looking forward to a rest, but, what happened? We were marched up and down the village main road to keep us occupied.

I reported to the medical officer about my knee, which was very painful, what did he do? He wrapped cotton wool around it and said I was okay to go marching and 'Fit for battle'. He was a bad one. He didn't give a toss about a man in pain, while he was comfortable back in his medical room.

It was about a week or two later and we'd assembled to go into the front line again. It was raining most of the time and I had the feeling of a temperature on me, just like when I had Bronchitis, in Norfolk the year before (I'd have repeats of a flu-like-feeling, now and again.). Of course, the constant rain made it worse. Well, I remember all of our company resting against a hedge, out of the rain and about twenty feet away, to the other side, were these woods where the bridge crossed a river.

Our sergeant picked my section, eleven men and him, and told us to get into a line ready to 'march' across this bridge. Well, we all nearly collapsed, "WHAT!", we said, "We can't do that. There's Germans over there!" He said, "Shut up! and do as your told, and you're to make as much noise as possible". Well, if eleven men had been told they were going to the electric chair to die, that's us!! We just couldn't believe it, but, go we had to, just like walking into a Lion's mouth. As we marched across to the other side, we were waiting to be cut to pieces by machine gun fire, just one machine gun would be enough and there was no escape for us. We marched on for about three hundred yards. I was on the end, next to the sergeant and I said to him, "That's far enough, if they were going to fire on us, they'd have done it by now.", "Ay, that's right." he said. Then he said "About turn!" Now we couldn't march fast enough get away from there and over the bridge to safety!

To think, the officers in command were willing to sacrifice twelve innocent lives, just to position us close to where the Germans were firing from, it's hard to believe and as I'm writing this down, it's making my hear beat faster.

We went back behind the hedge to shelter from the rain and we all lit up a fag each, but I felt too unwell to smoke, so I asked to see the medical officer. He examined me and my leg, he took my temperature and asked who'd put the bandage on my leg, I told him, then he told me I must get forty-eight hours rest at a camp. I couldn't believe my ears, next thing, a couple more men and me, were in an American Ambulance, being driven by a black soldier.

We were driving along a main road when the driver shouted "Man, What the hell is happening?" The whole sky and area was pitch black, the volcano, Vesuvius, had erupted and the ash had been thrown for miles around. It had covered the road with a couple of inches of ash. The driver had to stop and put his headlights on to stop any other vehicles from, blindly, running into him. Before we crossed the river, we noticed the flames shooting up out of the volcano and timed them as every three minutes. Now it had erupted.

We arrived at this muddy field, which was classed as a 'rest area', it was about three miles back from the front line. Well, at least we were out of it for a bit, so we could enjoy it. Another soldier and I had a two man 'Bivouac' to sleep in, a nice fellow, he was. We had good food there, as much a you wanted.

I was in the tent on my own in the day. I was praying to Our Lady to protect me and stop me going back in to the front line, I swear I saw an image of her appear before me. I was in a daze as if I had imagined it, but it remained in my mind for ever. I was not taking any medication so that was not the cause.

The chap who was in the same tent as me saw an Italian photographer coming around asking if anyone in the camp wanted their photograph taken. We had ours taken together because we didn't have enough money to have them taken separately. We had one full photograph of the two of us so we cut the photo down the middle and had our own individual photo as well. I have kept these until this day.

William Mark Lee

At rest camp for 48 hours. Two or more miles from the front line.

CHAPTER 17
THE FRONT LINE AGAIN, OR NOT

A jeep came to take me and another chap from our unit back to the front line. It was a sunny day and he dropped us off half a mile from the front line and drove away as fast as he could, as a shell could come over at any time. We started walking down a road towards the firing when a jeep came speeding towards us and away from the front of line. In the back was a brigadier, he stopped the jeep and said "Where the hell do you think you are going". We explained that we had been on a forty-eight hour rest and that we must now report to the nearest field hospital to see if we could rejoin our units.

The brigadier shouted "Don't you bother to report, just get back to the front line instantly because the Germans are breaking through our defences". No wonder he was going as fast as he could in the opposite direction. The chap with me had a big hole in the top of his leg from an abscess. I said to him "Take no notice of that brigadier, we'll report to the field hospital on the road nearby".

I reported to their medical officer and he looked at the dressing on my knee and asked if it was painful. I told him it was and that it had locked on me which made the pain worse. He said, "You will have to go back to No. 2 field hospital as I can not treat you here and it is dangerous for you to go back to your unit in the front line because if you're knee locks when you are up there you would be a burden to your unit". I couldn't have agreed more (thank God and his mother). The other chap was sent on to his unit, I felt so sorry for him walking alone down that horrific road.

After a short time an ambulance came from the front line direction to pick up the casualties from this station. I got in and right opposite me was a man from my section. His left hand bandaged, I said "What's happened to you" he replied that he was cleaning his rifle when it went off and blue three fingers of his left hand. I remember Ernie and me suggesting that we should shoot each other in the calf muscles but couldn't decide whether if it would have worked, and on another time, when the tanks were passing by, to put a foot or two under the tank tracks. Something had to snap within you to inflict a bad wound on your body, obviously this young soldier couldn't stand any more especially when the Germans had broken through the lines. He would now be sent to prison for a few years for self- inflicting wounds in the face of the enemy.

We arrived at the next, number 2, field hospital and following an examination they wrapped Elastoplast around my knee to hold it firm. They said "You will be able to go back to No. 3 field hospital and then on to No. 4". This was definitely a miracle to me. My medical records were marked 'I D K' and I thought this meant I don't know.

After a few days and after going further back, I eventually reached number 4 which was the last field hospital. At this point all the casualties were taken by stretcher on to an ambulance. I said I'd rather try and walk but this was not allowed. The ambulances took us to Naples dock and then on to a captured Italian hospital ship the "La Vita" there must have been a couple of hundred casualties on board.

When we had been at sea for a few days a rumour started to circulate that we were going back to Blighty (Britain) but we ended up in Algiers. It must have been about the first week of December 1943, it was pouring down as it was the wet season, when it rarely stopped raining.

I was in the last bed next to the flap in a large marquee. I was the only British soldier there, others were yanks and Canadians, not surprising as it was the 46th Canadian division in the Fifth American army in Italy. I heard them talking about how they enjoyed themselves when in Cardiff, of all places Cardiff.

On the 12th December 1943 I was 21 years old, what a birthday!. I had no one to even tell this to. A little Arab boy poked his head under the tent flap and looked at me and said "You buy dates". I had no money but I swapped a bar of soap for a small box of Algerian dates, happy 21st birthday Billy!!!.

After about a week I was admitted to the orthopaedic ward alongside many other patients waiting for operations. I knew I had the right to refuse an operation on my knee. It would not have been a simple cartilage operation as there was internal bone and ligament damage. I would have no guarantee that my leg would not be permanently stiff afterward, particularly if I had signed that the outcome was my responsibility. By the way 'I D K' stood for internal dislocation knee. What they would find when they opened my knee was anybody's' guess.

After a couple of days in the ward the surgeon came along looking at everyone's case and inspecting each chart at the bottom of each bed. The surgeon and his staff reached my bed looked at my chart and he said to the orderly "Get that man ready for surgery", they all started to walk away. I said "Excuse me sir" he turned around looked down his nose at me and said "Yes what do you want" I said, "Can you guarantee that I will not have a stiff leg after you've operated on my knee". "What!" he said, "of course I can't, I don't know what will happen afterwards". "Well", I said "In that case I am not going to have it done". They were all astonished with mouths wide of open in shock, he said "What did you say", and I repeated it. He was the last thing I was afraid of after what are I had gone through.

He turned to the orderly and shouted "Get that man out of here", the orderly told me that he had never heard anyone speak like that to the great orthopaedic surgeon, Sir something or other. So I didn't have the operation and was told to get dressed and go to another ward.

CHAPTER 18
BETTER DAYS AND XMAS DINNER - HAMEN LIF

A week or so afterwards, I went before two medical officers for grading from A1 (very fit) to B7 unfit for infantry duties, thank God no more front line for me. As I have stated before it was nothing but a miracle that my prayers were answered. I was transferred into the Royal army Service Corps R A S C. I was sent to a petrol serving company just outside Algiers in a village called Hamen Lif, an Arab village. We filled five gallon cans, with petrol, for transfer to the lorries and tanks. I learned to acetylene weld the bottom of the petrol cans (Jerry cans) if they were leaking so that they could be used again. It was a sitting down job naturally. It was a very hot job due to the heat from the welding torches and the stinking hot weather.

Algiers 1944

Algiers 1944

One day it was stifling hot because the Sahara wind was blowing, it was just like opening an oven door. The air was full of locusts, millions of them brought in by the wind. The Arabs were scooping them up into baskets and bags to take them home to fry and eat them. I was in that unit for about six months and then transferred to a bulk supply depot outside Naples. I enjoyed it in those easy units of the

R A S C considering that fighting was still going on in the North of Italy and Austria. Before I joined the supply depot outside Naples I was sent from of the petrol unit to a transit camp, where one goes while a unit is found for him. This transit camp had men from all units of the army infantry, artillery and so on.

It was on Christmas Day, we were in eight man tents and for meals we had a very large marquee. Christmas Day was the one day when officers serve Christmas dinner to the men. These officers were all from the Black Watch, a tough infantry unit. It was a lovely Christmas dinner and Christmas pudding and the top officer came with his young officers to every table asking if anyone wanted any more. No one would dare ask for more ordinarily but when he asked at our table I stood up and said "Yes thank you, I'd like some more". This very tall Scots man looked down at me, his black moustache bristling "What was that soldier", he said and I repeated myself. He then turned to the sergeant major and said "Did you hear what this man said" The Sergeant Major said to me "You've had your rations allotted to you and you

From the Back Streets to the Front Line

have the cheek to ask for more, do you realise there are men up the front line without any food what so ever today". I said "I know, I've been up there how about you?". As it was Christmas Day they wouldn't charge me for insolence so I got away with it.

Taken in Naples in 1944

So I was sent to this bulk supply depot where ships were unloaded at Naples dock and the food sent to the bulk supply depot to be distributed. The small food depot would collect food from us for rations to supply troop units in their areas. I met a chap called Ernie Turner who was from Ilkley Moor, Yorkshire and we stayed good mates till he was demobbed (sent home). This unit went to Padua and Verona. Although I was there I have forgotten these places. It was when I was visiting Naples with Ernie and another that we went to King Emmanuel's Palace. It had about seventy steps leading up to it. It had been turned into a N A A F I canteen and was a vast size inside with beautiful rooms.

Just before we went into the palace there was an Interflora flower shop just outside. I ordered a large spray or bouquet of flowers costing about 1 months pay, to be delivered to my mother on her birthday, January 1st 1944. My sister, Sheila, who was with my mother, told me when I came home on leave, years later, that the Interflora delivery man knocked on the door on the first of January and my mother said to the man "Oh no these can't be for me", until she looked at the note attached which read that it was from her loving son Bill. Sheila said that she was so excited she showed everyone in the street. That's something my mother must have been proud of.

She often sent me two hundred woodbines through an organisation like The Salvation Army, because they were everywhere, troops were. Mam would pay for them 'Duty Free' so they were a lot cheaper, but still cost money she couldn't afford. She regularly sent me letters (I only wished I'd kept them) and my sister, Mag, also sent me letters. It was to receive a letter and read of the family news. Mam insisted that I sent her a photo of me, every so often, so she could see for herself, how I was, she missed all of us so much. That's the reason I still have a few photos of me abroad in uniform.

I was in that unit for about six months. I went to visit our Tom, he was billeted in a monastery at Castle-Del-Mare. I was allowed to stay at his Billet for a weekend, he was in the Signal Corps, which was not far along the coast from Naples.

CHAPTER 19
VERONA - PADUA - GENOE - APPIANO - VIENA AND THE RUSSIANS

The next towns that I stayed at were Verona and Padua. We were travelling up Italy to keep supplying the troops, we were pushing the Germans out of Italy. I then stayed in Genoa, which I think was the thirty-eighth Bulk Supply Depot (B.S.D.). I enjoyed it in Genoa and went swimming in 'Mussolini's' palace swimming pool, I must have stayed there about twelve months and Ernie Turner was still with me.

Then I was moved to a lovely village called 'Appiano' near the Italian Alps. When it snowed the snow was always crisp, never 'slushy'. One time I borrowed a car this Corporal had, from a German soldier, and I took Ernie to the top of this mountain, the snow was quite deep. We had a glass or two of wine in this bar, it appeared to me that we were the first British soldiers to go up there. They didn't have to say it, they seemed afraid of us.

I said we'd better be down the mountain before dark because the small road was covered in snow. Halfway down, Ernie asked if he could drive the car down I said it was okay, because it was downhill all the way. Well, we went around this bend and then the car skidded and slid towards the edge of the road. I tried to pull it straight, luckily, the bumper hit a mile-stone, and it bounced back into the side of the road into a big snow drift. We had to dig it out by hand to get it going and get back to my Billets. One day, Ernie went away, He was demobbed so that was that.

Whilst stationed at Appiano in Italy a few of us were taken to a Ski resort in the mountains near Bolzano and it was full of skiers of all nations, we felt outsiders. We all tried skiing down a small hill and I ended up head first in the snow. We tried to go into the bars for a drink but they were crowded and far too expensive for us. It astounded me to see all these people enjoying themselves so soon after the war, only the rich could do this. We came back in the evening to our base at Appiano feeling dejected knowing those rich people would carry on enjoying themselves and we were still in the Army of occupation, for the like of them. We were eating sandwiches they were eating expensive meals and drinking wine whilst we watched outside. On another occasion I needed to visit a Dentist and the nearest one was in a German Army run Hospital about 10 miles away. I was told by my officer in charge to take a small German Volkswagen from some POW German officers in the camp. They played hell but I told them I was going to have it at a specific time tomorrow. The next day me and a German soldier collected the car and I drove it to the Hospital. On the way back the gear lever snapped off at the base with only an inch sticking out so I was stuck miles from anywhere and unable to use the gears. I had to hit the inch piece of lever into position and drive it all the way in second gear. Obviously the German Officers hack sawed the lever which they then had to repair for their own use.

I was based in an old mansion house, possibly the Lord of Appiano lived in it before the war. It was the biggest house in the area and it had a 7 foot high wall all around the grounds. It was about ¼ mile square and warehouses had been built by the German or Italian army to store the loot they had stolen like clothes, boots and shoes. We weren't allowed in these warehouses. There were about 30 British soldiers with around 12 to each bedroom. It was a good billet with good food, not like in the infantry with only a bare amount available. About 12 of us had a department for which to issue the troops rations, we had two German soldier helpers who were easy to get on with. One day an American soldier came to our depot asking our officers to allow him to stay with us until his own Army until could pick him up. They gave him food and a bed in our large bedroom where about 10 of us slept. The Yankee had bandages on his arms and ankles which he said were from an accident in the mountains with his vehicle. As we got into our beds, he slept next to me, I saw him put a handgun under his pillow. This made me very suspicious and I said to him "why the gun under your pillow, put it in your bag or you don't sleep near my bed you go outside to sleep". He then put it in his small back pack. He was a friendly guy and asked to come with me to the village Inns, he could speak German very well. So he came out drinking with me and my mates. When we came out of the Inn he pulled out his gun and started firing at the street lamps, outing them in the square. I told him to stop or he goes from our base so he did. I didn't like it one bit, the other fellows were terrified as they were not used to gunfire and the Yank thought he would frighten all of us so that he could stay in our camp undisturbed. He realised I wasn't afraid and he wanted to keep my company, he told me to come visit him in Texas but I ignored him. One day about a week later he left to go and stay in one of the Inns and that was the last I saw of him. A week later two military police came to see me at work and asked if I knew him and if I was a friend of his. I blew up and told them he was no friend of mine, they told me they had arrested him and he was in prison in Bolzano. Apparently he was an American deserter who belonged to a gang who stole train wagons of food to sell on the black market in Austria. Also, while he was in our camp he saw a lot of tyres against a wall down in the back of the warehouse. He went to Bolzano and met black market gangs and showed them where they were and arranged for their lorry to steal them by him passing them over the wall to them. He was paid millions of Lire and was living like a King in this small Inn. He had a big suitcase full of Lire notes under his bed when they arrested him. He was spending too much and the Military Police got to hear of it. He had told them he was a friend of mine, which I said was a lie. Apparently the bandages on his arms and ankles were covering big Syphilis sores. He was full of advanced Syphilis so it goes to show you must keep your eyes open always.

Now I was in the B.S.D I and was going to Vienna over the Italian Alps. Our Convoy left early one morning. I was in a small scout car that travelled up and down, while the Convoy was moving, just to make sure no bandits attacked the last vehicles and in case a vehicle stopped for any reason.

As we got to the top and started to cross along the flat the scout car that I was in stopped because one lorry was missing. We went back down and there was this stupid driver talking to two girls, an ideal trap set by road bandits on a last vehicle. We shouted at him and we followed him to the top, again, then along the flat top until we came to a fork road. Now, we couldn't see where our convoy had gone. We stood on top of the roof of the lorry but couldn't see a sign of which road to take so we took a left fork road. We drove on for about a half mile, when we came to a small archway of a bridge across the road. There was a sentry box on one side and from it ran two soldiers with machine guns pointed at us, Russian soldiers. We had to stop because they stood in the road and would have shot at us if we hadn't stopped. Now we realised we had come on the wrong road and were in trouble. They were savage, forcing guns at us and shouting to get us out of the vehicle, in Russian.

We had our hands in the air and spoke in English hoping they were friendly and could see we had made a mistake going there. They forced us into a group against the wall and we had to wait about half hour until a Russian officer came and escorted us into his town. All the whiles, the Russian soldiers were hanging onto the doors pointing machine guns at us.

We were all very nervous and worried. Not one of our convoy knew where we were so they wouldn't know where to look for us. In short these Russians could quite easily have kept us prisoners, for ever, as they have done to many British and German soldiers, so we were really frightened. The Russian officer, a short thin man with glasses, asked who the officer in charge of us was as they were suspicious. Were we deserters or were we spies sent to see how they were treating the people of that town. So one by one we were taken to a building and up the stairs to a dark room, escorted by a machine gunned Russian soldier. With a light on top of the desk I was placed in a big chair, the light shining in my face.

The Russian officer, I couldn't see him, started asking me to repeat what I had said to him before and why we had no officer with us. We all knew that we should not alter our story at all so we repeated the true reason for losing our convoy.

Me taken in Genoa in 1945

The people off the town came up to us when we were in the street, waiting to be called. They were so glad to see us and spoke good English. They asked if the British forces were taking over the town because of the Russians had been treating them badly. We told them that we knew of no such plans and they continued to tell us of the things the Russians did to them. We did not want to speak to them for long as we were being watched by the Russians. We did not want them to think that we supported these people as we simply wanted to get out of the town without delay.

After three or four hours with no food or drink the officer told us to get back into our vehicles and he would escort us out of the town. With Russian guards on the side of our lorries we were taken to the point at which we had entered the town and told to go fast before they changed their minds. We did, and we then knew that the other road lead us to the place we were heading, Vienna.

Somehow we found where our convoy was stationed and when we got there no one had known that we were missing. When the commanding officer heard about our capture he said we were lucky that he didn't put us on a charge for not following close to the convoy. As I had thought, no one would have known if the Russians had kept us, I shudder when I think of it.

I can't say how long we stayed in Vienna, a few of us all went horse riding in the Vienna woods and we also visited the Big Beer cellars. The Austrian lager was expensive but the very good.

CHAPTER 20
KLAGENFURT AND THE GERMANS

The next town that our unit moved to was called Klagenfurt and we were there until I was eventually demobbed. My service terminated in February 1947 so I had served five years, three and a half years abroad.

Klagenfurt is a bit hazy in my memory, every day from eight till five we supplied rations to the units in that area. I had a room in a long building in a courtyard with four German soldiers, they were prisoners of war, working for me. I was responsible for the contents in my store and for issuing rations that varied in size to each vehicle that came. My

Store served lard and hard biscuits, lard was like gold on the black market. We also issued dried beans and peas. I saw one of the Germans try to lift a container of biscuits to the window with difficulty. I told him to halt and put the container down, then I tried to lift it and found it was very heavy and when I opened it, it was full of lard. I was really annoyed because they were stealing a piece of lard from each ration and saving it to sell on the black market.

They pleaded with me to forgive them for stealing and asked me not to report them as they would be sent to prison. I kept quiet and made them give all the lard back by adding a little to each ration. I could not keep it in the store, so it was given back to the ones it was stolen from. One of them, Otto, spoke good English, I got on well with them in general, they looked up to me afterwards.

Every morning at 10 o'clock break I would be given a thick steak in a sandwich of fresh bread which one of the Germans got for me from the Germans working in the butcher store and the cook house.

I found the German soldier was no different from a British soldier, in fact you could say we were 'Brothers', they didn't want war, Hitler and The Nazi movement did.

CHAPTER 21
GETTING OUT

Well, at last I could go home on a fortnights leave, after three years abroad. This would be about the beginning of 1946. A couple of us went. We were driven to 'Villack' to a train station. Hundreds of us were on the train that went through France to the port of Calais, onto a small ship, then arrived at Dover or Folkestone. On the way over a warning come over the Tannoy, that if anyone was found with German or Italian hand guns, they would be sent back to Austria and prison. Well, the guns that were pushed through the porthole must have been over a hundred. Everyone wanted to get home, even if it was only for a fortnight.

It was quite strange while on the tube train, to hear a little girl speak English to her Mam. That was the first time for nearly three years, that I'd heard that. Well, my Mam and family and the rest of the street, were at their front doors, watching me walk down the street. My Mam ran up the street, towards me, arms outstretched, someone had seen me coming from the station and had run and told everybody.

The fortnight went quickly and dull, I'm afraid, all my work mates were still in the forces, so I was glad, in a way, to get back. Everyone was still on strict rations, not like I had in our Depot in Austria.

Eventually I was demobbed when we arrived at Folkestone, we were taken to a big shed that had these counters with shirts, ties, suits, etc which were all civilian clothes. We went in a soldier and came out a civilian.

I had over three months leave coming to me, one day for every month abroad. My intention was to go to South Africa on a Government ground nut scheme to produce oil from the peanuts that the natives would collect, we 'whites' would supervise them.

My friend from Marks and Spencer, Howard Evans, said he would come, so I delayed applying. After two months, I could see he didn't intend to go. By then I'd started back in Marks and Spencer, and was back in a groove that I was in before I was called up.

It must have been fate, because I saw a red headed girl in the staff dept. who really interested me. When I asked her to go out with me, she always said no, yet, any other girl I asked out, would say yes. I couldn't settle, working indoors, so I left that job for an outdoor job, on the railway in Cathays yard. That didn't suit me either. I still wanted to go abroad, but the government ground nut scheme had ended, so I was stuck in Cardiff.

A miracle, it seems, stopped me from the terrible carnage at Salerno. I was protected when I was in danger in the front line in Italy, as I've written, firstly a sniper's bullet hit my helmet, a bit lower and it would have gone through my head. Then, the machine gun bullets went alongside me, sitting outside my mate's pit. Then, the German who was firing our machine gun down on us, but was blown up by the hand grenade the Lance Corporal threw at him. Then, I thought I'd seen Our Lady after I'd been sent back from the line, on forty-eight hours rest.

A lot of my mates were killed when our company did across over that bridge, when I was sent back to the rest of the camp. Although I was sent back into the front line with a really painful knee by the Medical Officer I was somehow fated to go to that Medical first aid post even though at that point I was very close to being in the front line. From then on I was sent further and further back away from the front line until I reached Algiers. I believe without any doubt that I was protected and saved so that I could later meet Hilda Morgan, who needed my protection. Together we produced a loving Catholic family as I think God would have it. He set the task for the two of us and gave us the love, the will and strength to succeed. That is a rather recent chapter of my life and I will not relate to it any further other than it was very difficult. Similar to a lot of people

From the Back Streets to the Front Line

when we were young no one had money. To obtain the money to survive one had to work very hard, and this was called 'Britain a land fit for Heroes', codswallop!.

18 years old 1940

Printed in the United Kingdom
by Lightning Source UK Ltd.
133959UK00001B/63/P